The *GOLF Magazine* Course Management Handbook

The *GOLF Magazine* Course Management Handbook

Gary Wiren, Ph.D.
PGA Master Professional
and the Editors of *GOLF Magazine*

The Lyons Press

First Lyons Press edition, 1999

Printed in the United States of America
Design and composition by Compset, Inc.

10 9 8 7 6 5 4 3 2 1

Library of Congress Cataloging-in-Publication Data

Wiren, Gary.
    The GOLF magazine course management handbook/
Gary Wiren and the editors of GOLF magazine. —1st
Lyons Press ed.
        p. cm.
    ISBN 1-55821-809-2 (pbk.)
    1. Golf—Handbooks, manuals, etc. I. GOLF mag-
azine. II. Title.
GV965.W723 1999
    796.352'3—dc21   99-18227
                                                      CIP

Contents

Foreword

At *GOLF Magazine* we use two methods to determine the content of each issue: surveys and guts. In the survey method, questionnaires are sent to thousands of subscribers, asking—among other things— what topics they enjoy most and which kinds of articles they prefer. In the guts method, we editors simply use our intuition as kindred, hopelessly addicted golfers.

But no matter which method we use, the number one request is always for the same thing: instruction. "Give us more instruction" has been the mandate from our readers ever since the magazine began publishing, forty years ago. The reason is simple: A golfer is happiest when his game is improving.

Recently, however, we've learned a couple of things about how to present our instruction. First, you like it short and sweet. After all, most of the current population were raised on television, sound bites, and quick delivery of information—from beepers to e-mail. More than ever, we like our messages short and to the point.

And the "to the point" part is just as important as the "short" part. For the last decade or so, the most popular portion of *GOLF Magazine* has been the buff-colored section, "Private Lessons," which brings together custom-tailored instruction for five different kinds of golfers: low handicappers, high handicappers, short but straight hitters, long but crooked hitters, and senior golfers. In this way, we're able to speak more personally with our readers and help them more individually with their games.

Why am I telling you all this? Because the same kind of thinking went into the book that is now in your hands. When the people at the Lyons Press came to talk to us about a partnership in golf-book publishing, we gave them our mantra for success: instruction, succinct and focused. The result is the *GOLF Magazine* series of guides, each written concisely, edited mercilessly, and dedicated entirely to one key aspect of playing the game.

Each *GOLF Magazine* guide assembles a wealth of great advice in a package small enough to carry in your golf bag. We hope you'll use these pages to raise your game to a whole new level.

—George Peper
Editor-in-Chief
GOLF Magazine

The *GOLF Magazine* Course Management Handbook

Introduction

When I am asked, "What does it take to play winning golf?" my reply is always the same. It takes six elements: 1) sound technique, 2) physical conditioning, 3) mental strength, 4) proper equipment, 5) regular practice, and 6) sound course management, all of which are touched upon in this series of books to improve your game. While the first five generally capture more attention in the media, the sixth, course management, is just as important and in some cases even more so. I have worked with players, even at the Tour level, who had mastered the first five yet never reached their potential because they failed the challenge of course management. They knew how to hit the ball, but they were still learning how to play the game. If you are talking "winning golf," number six is one element you can't overlook.

What Is Good Course Management?

Good course management means playing smart golf; not smart as in IQ smart but rather as in commonsense smart. A Ph.D. is really of little value on

Academically smart does not necessarily translate to "golf smart."

the golf course. At its best, good course management means being able to curve the ball and manage trajectory when you need to; knowing your game, such as your club distances and shot tendencies; knowing how to handle various lies and situations on the course; how to cope with poor weather conditions; understanding risk and reward; and finally, controlling your attitude and emotions in competitive situations. All of these will be covered in the following pages. Plus, you will be given a simple six-item guide at the end, "The Stroke-Saver System," which in itself is invaluable for doing just what it says for your game, save strokes.

A Valuable Lesson

It was forty years ago: I was a graduate student in Ann Arbor, Michigan, when I got some of the best advice I have ever heard on playing winning golf. I had just finished eighteen holes at the tough University of Michigan Blue Course, an Alister Mackenzie design, and had again been beaten out of a few bucks by a middle-aged part-time Tour caddie with whom I played on occasion. It was always a shock to me, because he didn't have nearly the distance I did, nor as good a swing, and certainly not the quality of my playing equipment. *But*

The player with a great short game is a match for anyone.

he sure had my number. We sat in the snack bar afterward and over a soft drink he said, "Gary, let me tell you about winnin' golf. First you drive the ball somewhere out there where you can find it; after that you knock it up there on, or around, the green, *and then the game she really starts.*"

Having the ability to get up and down from around the green is one skill all serious players appreciate.

My opponent was absolutely right: He knew the value of keeping the ball in play and having a great short game. But what he failed to share with me at that time was the wisdom, the tricks, and the management of himself and his game that made that philosophy work. This book contains much of what he didn't tell me, the things that I have had to learn since he took my few student dollars. And oh how I wish I had known these stroke-saving course management techniques sooner in my golf life. I didn't, but at least I can share them with you now to give you a short cut on your march to a better game.

Two "Greats" on Management

If someone asked you to name the greatest golfer of all time you could return a variety of answers. Based on the record, however, there can be only one: Jack Nicklaus. His 81 PGA and Senior Tour victories, 28 major wins, and 58 second-place finishes support that choice. The interesting fact is with that impressive record he still never won any of the individual statistical titles (i.e., fewest putts, longest average drive, sand saves, greens in regulation, etc.). So while he wasn't the best at producing specific shots, he was the best at playing the game. *His fellow competitors always conceded Jack the title of smartest player, which translates to "best course manager."*

Another all-time great, Sam Snead, once wrote a book with Al Stump called *The Education of a Golfer*. Sam related many experiences from his career and then, at the end of each chapter, shared stroke-saving thoughts for the average player. Part of the book's premise was that Sam could walk eighteen holes with twenty-plus handicap players and cut five to six strokes off their score by simply coaching them to manage their game and thoughts in a golf-smart way.

Throughout the book Sam discusses situations where a player should use a 3 wood rather than

A lower-viewing perspective reveals the slope more accurately, particularly on the greens.

the driver from the tee; and where a 7 iron chip and run is a higher percentage choice than a sand wedge pitch. He provides other great tips as well, including how a positive frame of mind and seeing good pictures before the swing reduces tension; how to aim

away from trouble; and a better procedure for read-
ing putts. The result when these coaching tips were
put into practice invariably produced a lower score.
*So take it from two of the greatest golfers who have played
the game and proven it by their results: Good golf is smart
golf . . . and here is how you do it.*

A Game of Control

Being in control defines smart golf. That includes *shot-making control, decision-making control, and emotional control.* Smart golf is also adapting to what you can't control, such as the performance of your opponent, the weather, course conditions, or the bounces that the ball takes, good and bad. Anyone who has played competitive golf, at either the club level or Tour level has experienced an opponent (like my Michigan acquaintance) who doesn't have a particularly good swing, can't hit it very far, doesn't impress you with any particular part of his/her game, yet manages to win the match. That opponent seemed composed, rarely made a mistake, and when he did, managed to somehow recover. It was like the opponent possessed an advanced degree in scrambling.

Green speed is a condition you don't control. You have to adapt to it.

But what he really had was a thorough knowledge of how to use his experience, intelligence, and good judgment to produce the most effective shots and make the fewest errors. What they own is course management skill. They are in control.

Ball Flight Laws

If we accept the fact that smart golf is golf that is in control then what is it we have to control? The most important thing is the ball. So good course managers have a clear understanding of the factors that influence ball flight.

What are the elements of ball control over which you have some influence? These elements can be described using the five laws of ball flight from the model **Laws, Principles and Preferences:**[*] 1. Clubhead speed; 2. centeredness of contact; 3. swing path; 4. clubface alignment; and 5. angle of clubhead approach.

Clubhead speed is the most important of the laws of ball flight in producing distance, assuming the other four are reasonably correct. If you don't know your clubhead speed, it can be accurately measured by training aid products that range from simple clip-on devices to sophisticated electronic

---

[*]The model, Laws, Principles and Preferences was created by the author in 1978 and is a part of the *PGA Teaching Manual*, 1990. It presents a three-tiered description of the mechanics of ball flight that the player can influence by his/her application of fundamentals, or **principles,** and technique, or style, labeled as **preferences.**

A club held upside down and swung to create a *whooshing* sound
is a good speed indicator. The louder the sound the better.

instruments. You can work on increasing clubhead speed using auditory feedback. In other words, just by listening. When making a practice swing hold the club at the neck end, swing it, and listen for a *whooshing* sound. The greater the speed the louder the sound. You'll discover that lighter grip pressure, particularly in the right hand, will help increase the sound. *Feeling like you are going to "sling" it rather than "hit it" will create lighter grip pressure and increase clubhead speed.*

Centeredness indicates where on the clubface you make contact with the ball: toe, heel, high or low. Any contact made away from the center will reduce distance and can contribute to misdirection as well. An easy way to determine where on the face you are making contact is by applying stick-on face decals. You'll be surprised how often you don't hit the center of the clubface (a good testimonial for perimeter-weighted clubs). *Your best center-face hits will come with correct ball position and arms and hands that stay extended without tension during the swing.*

The **swing path** on which the clubhead is traveling through impact is one of the two most important factors influencing the ball flight direction. The

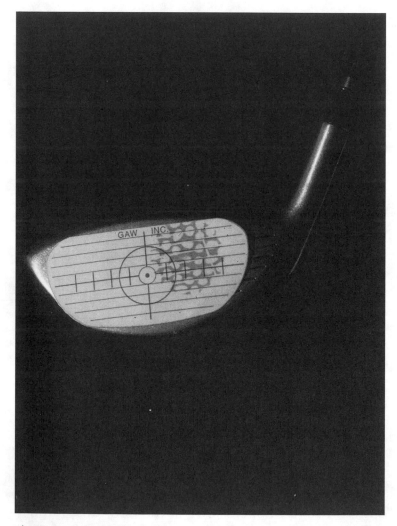

This impact decal shows that the shot was hit in the heel, probably losing about eight to ten yards in distance from a normal 240-yard drive.

path can be influenced by many factors: where you aim your body; the sequence of forward motion through impact; and your intentional arm and hand swing direction to a target. Developing a consistent swing path is one of the most important tasks a golfer can undertake to become a good player. *Much of the success or failure of your swing path will be the result of your body alignment and ball position before the swing ever starts.* There are several commercial alignment devices on the market that could help. But one of the easiest and most convenient methods to improve your body alignment is to put parallel clubs on the ground to identify your target line and foot line. You may have seen or heard that recommendation a thousand times before, but don't take it lightly. It is simple but effective. Once the clubs are in position, aim your hips and shoulders parallel to those lines, and on the forward swing follow that parallel image of your shoulder line.

The next ball flight law, **clubface alignment** (known hereafter simply as "face"), is the single greatest contributor to the shot direction and shape. At impact the face will either be open, closed, or square to your swing path, determined largely by one's grip; or by the left wrist position

The learning aid, Impact Bag, gives accurate feedback on where the club and body should be at the moment of truth, at impact.

(for right-handers) at the top of the swing; or by the amount of forearm and hand rotation, called "release." Timing the face to be square is one of the great challenges of producing accurate shots. *The most effective tool we use in teaching the position is an Impact Bag,* which captures the clubhead in the forward swing and freezes the position of the body.* The soft resistance of the bag gives kinesthetic feedback to the player so he or she can identify the correct body, arm, and hand positions that produce square clubface contact. This correct impact position is repeated until it becomes habit.

The final ball flight law, the **angle of approach,** affects the trajectory of a shot. For example, on a pitch shot or bunker shot if you simply steepen the backswing by cocking the wrists abruptly, you'll produce a sharper angle of swing descent resulting in a higher shot. You get a similar but unwanted result when skying a wood shot (too steep a descent from activating your hands prematurely).

Also, the steeper the descent on a full shot, like a drive, the greater amount of backspin is created to lessen its overall distance. The shallower the club-

---

*See reference at end of book.

Learning to place the hands on the club correctly is one of a player's most important tasks.

head approach the more the force is directed to the target, resulting in less backspin and greater distance. You can practice this shallower approach by holding your club in the air about two feet above the ball and making baseball-like practice swings as though going after a low pitch. Then tilt forward at the hips until you assume your normal address position and make a similar swing at the ball. *This modified baseball swing practice will help re-*

*duce the angle of steepness in the clubhead's approach to
the ball.*

You have just been introduced to the five ball flight
laws and suggestions for improving technique in applying them. Understanding this information provides you with the fundamental physics behind ball
flight. This is the foundation for shot control. Now
let's look more closely at strategies for making these
shots and playing the course.

Shot Control—Understanding Cause and Effect

While golfers cannot completely control their
shots, they ought to know the technique necessary
to make the ball go high, low, left to right or right
to left, longer or shorter when applied correctly. To
be most effective in course management a player
must be able to exert this kind of control over his or
her shots.

Shot Shape

Intentionally curving a golf ball can be accomp-
plished by having some knowledge of simple geom-

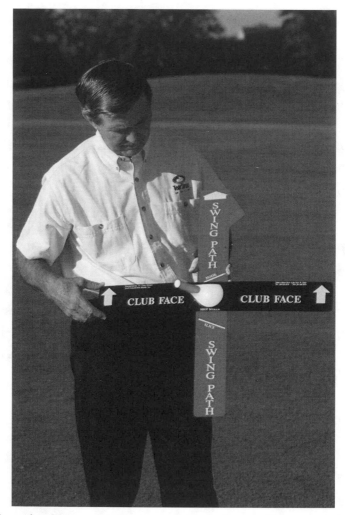

When the face and path are at right angles as demonstrated by this learning aid—called the "Shot Maker"—the ball will travel straight.

ctry and physics and applying it. Shaping a golf shot is a skill that can certainly come in handy when you need a ball to go around a tree or some other obstacle. Honestly, it is not that hard! *By combining the two elements of clubface alignment and swing path you can create almost any amount of curve that you desire.* Whenever the swing path and clubface line up to make a *right angle* (geometry), no matter in what direction the swing path is going, then the principle resultant *vector force* (physics), the ball's directional flight and velocity, is projected forward along the path the clubhead is taking. If that path is to the right the shot will be a push, to the left a pull.

When the face and path are not at right angles, the ball is struck a glancing blow causing sidespin, which makes the ball curve. If the face is open to the path for right-handed players the ball will curve to the right. If slightly open it will be a fade, or if more open, a slice. When the face is slightly closed to the path, it will produce a draw; when more closed, a hook. *Where the ball starts is generally determined by the path of the swing and where it curves by the face.*

There is, however, the possibility of "clubface override." This can happen when the swing path travels to the right of the target line (from inside to out) yet the

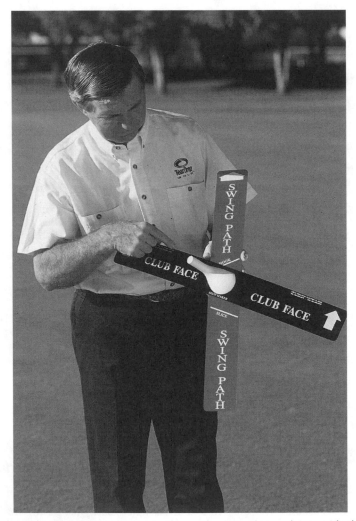

When the clubface is open to the path, as is shown here with the Shot Maker, the ball will slice.

ball starts to the left of the target line. Such an event is the result of a dramatically closed clubface. An example of this would be if the path is 4 degrees to the right but the face is looking 8 degrees to the left. The same holds true with a swing that goes to the left of target (outside to in). With a clubface position grossly open, the ball will not start to the left but rather to the right of the swing path line. In other words, the face position "overrides" the path.

This is a demonstration of "clubface override" in which the starting path of the ball will reflect the position of the club face and not swing path. If the club face is closed, as shown here, the ball will start left.

You can practice shaping the ball and test your path and face combinations by placing a target marker about thirty yards in front of you, where it is easy to trace the starting path and shot shape. Experiment with different swing paths and different face positions to discover how the combinations work. *Path is most easily changed by the alignment of*

An umbrella has been placed in the ground to use as a reference point around which to shape the ball flight.

feet and more important, shoulders. Your club swing path will naturally want to follow your shoulder alignment. The clubface can be preset to an open or closed position, always aiming to where you want to finish. The amount you open or close it will depend upon how much curve you desire. This shaping skill can come in very handy on the course and is not really hard to do (see illustration). In addition, it will help you to understand why your unintentional curves happen.

Trajectory

In the quest for better scoring, it is a great advantage to be able to control the trajectory (height) of your shots; low under obstacles or when playing into the wind and high over barriers or for soft landings on the greens. *There is one principle that controls trajectory other than the loft built into the club; it is the relationship of the grip end to the clubhead end, or the angle of shaft tilt.* The more the grip end is tilted forward, ahead of the clubhead, the lower the trajectory. The farther back the grip end is leaned the higher the shot will travel.

Moving the ball back in the stance at address will naturally tilt the shaft toward the target. This is the way most players create lower trajectory shots. The

Foreword tilt of the clubshaft at impact translates to lower flight.

The more vertical the shaft becomes the higher the ball flight.

Try using trees and mounds when practicing trajectory control.

reverse holds true when you move the ball forward and tilt the shaft to more vertical, giving the ball a higher trajectory. Adjusting the ball position at address is not a guarantee of trajectory since you could play the ball back in an attempt to hit it low and make an early release of the hands. This scooping-style swing negates the original forward leaning shaft angle, possibly even causing it to have a backward lean, which sends the ball high rather than low. So while ball position helps to bring about the desired result, in fact it is the lean of the shaft at impact that really counts.

To practice trajectory control go to the side of the practice area where there may be some trees and experiment with different ball positions and impact shaft angles in trying to play shots under and over branches. This is one of the easier principles to learn and apply.

Decision-Making Control— Knowing Your Game and the Course

One of the mistakes that causes a player to make poor decisions is allowing the ego to entice him/her into trying to match the shot making of a superior ball-striking partner or opponent. Golf matches and tournaments aren't always won by the best ball striker. On the contrary, in matches of reasonably equal talent, winning golf is more often the product of knowing and staying within one's circle of competence; in other words, doing what you know you can do and not attempting the heroic. Playing "your game" is achieved by knowing what you can do and making good decisions after the important factors have been considered. Unlike some of the other vagaries of golf, the decision-making process is one over which the player does have complete control. The question then becomes, "How well do you know your own game?"

Getting the Distance

Golf is a game of both distance and direction, with control of distance being an important part of the equation. *If you don't know the distances you hit your clubs—and most golfers honestly don't (they tend to overestimate)—then you are giving away a lot of shots on the course.* How far do you hit your 5 iron, driver, or pitching wedge? Is the yardage figure you come up with all carry or does it include roll? Does your answer represent "your best ever" distance or your average distance?

For example, if there is a bunker at the corner of a dogleg 237 yards away, can you carry it in the air? Or let's say you are trying to play safe and not roll into the long grass fronting the green on a par five hole. The distance to the grass is 218 yards: Do you know what to hit? How about a shot to the green that is over water that extends right to the front of the putting surface; the carry is 174 yards with the flagstick eight steps back; do you know the right club? Having an accurate knowledge of how far your iron shots to the green carry and tend to roll also makes a world of difference in how long your putts will be. Face up to the fact that the length of your first putt on the green correlates directly with how many putts you are going to take. The statistics from touring professional players indicates that from 6 feet they make roughly 65 percent, from 12 feet 32 percent, and from 30 feet only 12 percent. And for amateurs, the percentage is surely much poorer. *Isn't that in itself enough reason to learn your club distances?*

So how do you learn your distances? When teeing off with a driver, make note of where you are playing from in relation to the permanent tee marker and the length of the hole. Let's say it is a 385 yard par four. When you arrive at your ball, seek out the nearest fairway sprinkler head or other distance markers to see how far you have remaining to the center of the green and subtract it from the total distance of the hole to determine your driving distance. This won't tell you the carry for the drive unless the fairways are unusually soft and your ball has made a plug mark, in which case you can also determine the carry from the mark.

A more techno-centered means of finding your length with each club is to use an electronic distance-measuring device. You may find these at such places as indoor playing and club fitting centers; golf learning-aids catalogs or in specialty golf stores; and handheld electronic range finders that can be taken on the course. Indoor golf centers tend to have their machines "jacked up" to make the clients feel good, so a realistic outdoor measurement may be more accurate. One tool that is right on the money for distance that you can acquire and take with you when you play is the Bushnell 600 Range Finder, an optical monocular high-quality instrument, accurate within a yard up to 600 yards.[*]

Electronic tools aside, the more traditional way to get your distances for irons and sometimes even

---

[*]See reference at end of book.

The Bushnell 600 is excellent for getting your yardage on the course and on the practice range.

fairway woods has been to monitor shots on the par-three holes. A permanent marker in the ground or a post should indicate the distance to the center of the green from that spot. Step off the distance from the marker to the location of the tee blocks to be accurate. Add or subtract yardage as needed. Hit your shot, then check your result in relation to the center of the green, not to where the flagstick is located. Also on iron shots to the green, pay close attention to the fairway sprinkler heads and the permanent 100-, 150-, and 200-yard markers. Take your steps from them to your ball, add or subtract yardage, and then note what clubs you need to get to the green. Find where your pitch mark is on the green to determine carry and roll.

Half Shots

Knowing correct distances also applies to less than full shots. In fact, these shots are often more difficult because they require judgment for the swing length and effort. That's why you may hear good players talk about "laying up" on a par-five to play from a distance where they can take a full swing rather than getting closer and be faced with a half shot where more touch is required. How much shorter does your ball go when you choke down on the grip by one inch, two inches? In my own case, it is ten yards for every one and a half inches. How far do you take the club back to hit a thirty- to forty- or fifty- to sixty-yard wedge shot? This question can be answered in a couple of good practice sessions by doing the following: Go to a practice area and measure off distances in ten-yard increments from thirty to sixty yards, placing a marker at each location. Take your sand wedge, or whatever club you use for that length, and hit balls to

Practicing distance control with a sand wedge.

each successive target, noting the length of backswing it takes to produce the correct distance.
When former Open champion Tom Kite has a full
pitch shot and asks his caddie how far they are
from the flag, he doesn't accept a comment like,
"About forty-five yards." He wants to know, "Is it
forty-six or forty-four?" That precision comes from
having measured the distances in practice and frequently rehearsing the swing length to have the
feel of how to make it happen.

The Target

Once you know how far the ball goes with each club (full swing, half swing) then it's important to know for sure how far the target is from your ball. We have mentioned permanent markers and sprinkler heads in the fairways as well as the permanent marker on the tee ground. It is important to understand that on a par-three hole the scorecard distance and the actual playing distance are very seldom the same. How far away are the tee markers from the hole's permanent marker as printed on the scorecard? How many yards or steps are the tees in front or behind the permanent marker? What is the flagstick location today in relation to the center of the green? Are you going to have to either add or subtract yardage? Is the green uphill or downhill from the tee area? This could make a difference from a half club to maybe even two clubs; it will require more club for uphill and less for downhill. Is there a wind that will help or hurt? Will you need to increase or decrease one, two or even three clubs to compensate for it? A crosswind also will affect the distance of your shot, depending upon which side it is coming from and whether you draw the ball or fade your shots. If you *consider all these factors you can then come up with the actual "play-*

ing distance" for the hole, not the scorecard distance. Finally, where is the most severe trouble on the hole? Is it over the green, in the front, or on the side? If you judge incorrectly, would it be better to be too long or too short to miss on the right or the left? On

This is the kind of shot where distance control is critical.

the par-three 15th at PGA National in Palm Beach Gardens, Florida, which is fronted by water, you don't want to be short. In different years, both Don January and Ray Floyd left it short and it cost them respective PGA Seniors' Championships; one making five, the other a seven. For safety's sake it is wise to use more club than normally necessary if the penalty for being short is severe. The reverse (use less club) is true if there is a penalty for being long. It all goes into the equation known as "club selection," an important part of good golf course management.

Percentages

Given five shots with a driver to a fairway that is less than thirty yards wide with trouble on both sides, how often do you feel you can place your ball into that space? There are times in a golf round when such a shot is required. If your answer is one out of five with a driver, but three out of five with a fairway wood, then you'd better play the percentages and hit the fairway wood. If on a par-five, the carry over the water on your second or third shot is 215 yards and you can hit your 3 wood a maximum of 220, then what are the odds that you will hit it perfectly? If on another hole the flag is tucked behind a bunker, it's a firm green, you are downwind and playing a hard two-piece ball, do you go for the pin or to the open part of the green where you can land short and bounce the shot on? *A golf round gives you lots of opportunities to make decisions like these, and these decisions should take percentages into consideration.*

The reason that Las Vegas can build multimillion-dollar casinos is because people who go there are willing to take a gamble, even when the odds in the long run are never in their favor. Therefore, they lose more often than they win. When you are on the golf course, leave the gambling to Vegas unless the odds are in your favor or the risk-to-reward ratio is worth it. Consistency is golf's toughest challenge and reckless gamblers on the course are seldom consistent. When you are going to attempt a high-risk shot ask yourself, "Am I comfortable or nervous making this attempt?" and "Do I believe I could pull it off three out of four times if given the chance?" If your answers tell you to go, then go, providing the risk is worth it. Keep in mind, however, that more often than not, it isn't worth the risk.

Tendencies

Another factor to consider is your tendency under a given circumstance. Let's assume that you are

Do you risk it? Make your decision based upon the odds, the circumstance, and your personal history.

playing a 165-yard par-three with a green surrounded by water except on the left where there is a bail-out area. The flagstick is on the right-hand side of the green near the water and the wind is blowing strongly left to right. The odds for hitting a good shot may be reasonable; you may even feel good about your chances of getting close. But if your historical tendency in that situation is to push-fade the ball because you tighten up, then you'd better take that into consideration. Aim left where there is enough margin for error that a push-fade would still hit the green and where a straight shot may miss the green but give you an easy chip. The point is, you have taken the water out of play by acknowledging your tendencies.

Self Control

Another factor to consider is your behavior in certain playing situations. For example: Do you press for more distance when playing with long hitters, only to find you lose control and shoot higher scores? Have you recognized that when playing with better players, particularly pros, you rush your shots to get out of the way? Does being held up on the course because of slow play irritate you to the point where you get upset and it affects your game? Does playing with people about whom you don't particularly care change your normal approach to the game and cause you to lose focus? These are cases in which you need to control yourself more than control the ball. *If you have a tendency to let these kinds of circumstances negatively affect your performance, then you must either avoid them when possible, or acknowledge them and adopt a strategy to overcome them.*

Handling Course Conditions

Equally important to knowing your game is knowing *the* game, which means knowing how to handle course conditions.

A golf course presents a monumental test of one's ability to handle varied conditions. Think for a moment of the possibilities: wind, rain, cold, heat;

Being able to "read" bunker sand (having a feeling for how the ball will come out) is part of the course management learning process.

up-, down-, and sidehill terrain; deep grass, short grass, and no grass; fast, slow, grainy, undulating, flat, and wet greens; tight, narrow, and sloping fairways; elevated, downhill, and around-the-corner targets; fine and coarse bunker sand with various depths; trees and bushes, lakes, rivers and oceans, they all add up to challenging your adaptability, creativity and courage— qualities of a good course manager.

Wind

Wind is the most common weather element we face on a golf course. The fact that it comes from different directions and at different velocities during a round, or even during one hole, makes for some interesting adjustments.

When playing into the wind off the tee many players try to hit harder. But attempting extra distance will likely cause you to lose control. This mistake is made even worse because ball flight errors are really magnified in heavy winds. A typical shot that would curve ten yards off line under calm conditions will deviate only five yards when hit downwind but twenty-five yards when stuck into a strong headwind. Trajectory is critical, since you want to keep the ball lower, to get under the wind. Most players when playing into the wind attempt to keep the ball down by tee-ing the ball lower on wood shots. However, this can be counterproductive, as it tends to steepen your angle of approach to the lower teed ball, thereby adding backspin. This type of swing produces what is known as a "riser," or ball that starts low and climbs abruptly but then drops with little forward roll. It is not a strong shot into the wind. A shallower or more level angle of approach using any tee height will produce a greater vector force traveling toward the target and a ball with less backspin. That is why you will sometimes see a player competing in a long-drive competition teeing the ball high, even into the wind, seeking a more level swing.

When playing iron shots to the green you can keep the ball lower and under a heavy wind by simply taking a club with less loft and either short-ening your hand position on the grip or limiting your backswing. Either of these adjustments will affect distance control. Taking a stronger club than you would normally think to use when hitting into the wind is almost always a good idea, since the tendency, even for professionals, is to not use enough club. Remember that a drawing or hooking ball will fight the wind better because the trajectory will generally be lower. More important, it will have less backspin.

This shot into the wind is being played with a restricted backswing to help keep the trajectory down.

When hitting a tee shot with the wind behind you (a following wind), the lift and drag are reduced and so is the trajectory. In order to achieve the optimum trajectory you may need to tee the ball higher. To get optimum distance from a side wind, shape the shot to ride the wind rather than playing one that fights it. This is because riding the wind reduces drag.

Rain

The Boy Scouts' motto, "Be Prepared," is a good place to start when considering the challenges to scoring that weather presents. Rain is one of the most common and most difficult conditions. Being prepared for

A large golf umbrella is a necessity for the frequent player.

rain means having a sixty-two-inch golf umbrella; two large towels that you keep dry by carrying them under your umbrella struts or in the golf car; at least three extra golf gloves; a rain suit that is truly waterproof; a rain hat (one with a broad brim if you wear glasses); waterproof shoes; a nonslip grip product that can be used on your grips if they get slippery in wet weather or a special glove that grips better when wet; and a hood for your golf bag to keep rain from going inside. If you are in a golf car without a cover attached to the back, restrap your bag so it doesn't stand vertically but rather hangs out to the side where the water won't as easily run down into it and get your grips wet. Do this maneuver by pulling the cart strap through the bag handle and angling your clubs off to the side. If you choose to do this, be more careful driving the car, since your clubs are "sticking out." The best situation is to have a cover that goes over the entire car, including your clubs.

That keeps everything and everybody protected from the elements. The number one rule is, *whatever it takes, keep your hands and the grips on your clubs dry.*

Shot making needs to be adjusted for rain as well. You will not get your normal distance for several reasons, such as: wet ground that cuts down

Hanging your clubs to the side, then using a towel over them, will help keep rainwater from getting on the grips.

roll; wearing extra clothing that may hamper your swing; and the rain itself creating "heavier air." Don't try to press for extra distance from the tee or in the fairway, as the wet conditions make it easier to produce errors during your swing. Trying to hit harder will only exacerbate the situation. And certainly don't expect your normal distance when playing from wet, heavy rough. Just get the ball out and back to the fairway.

There is one instance during wet conditions where the loss of distance is reversed. When water gets between your clubface and the ball, reducing the amount of backspin, the result is known as a "flier," a shot that travels farther than normal. This commonly happens when your ball is resting in light rough and the wet blades of grass "grease" the clubface to make the ball shoot forward on a lower, "hotter" trajectory, with less backspin to stop it once it hits the ground. However, "fliers" can happen in any wet condition, not just from the rough. If you anticipate the "flier" possibility you can use one less club (a 6 iron rather than a 5) or you can swing with less effort than normal.

Combating Cold

Two other common weather hazards are extreme cold or heat. *For cold weather preparation, focus on the warmth of your hands, feet, and head.* Carry gloves for keeping your hands warm in between shots, a handwarmer in your pocket, a cold weather hat or cap, and either an extra pair of regular socks or thermal socks. Wear loose-fitting clothes that don't hamper your swing, preferably those that are tested for their thermal effectiveness. Carry two extra golf balls in your warmest pocket and rotate them with the one in play on every other hole. Cold golf balls do not go as far as warm golf balls because the material from which the ball is made does not respond as efficiently as it gets colder. A shot that travels 200 yards at 70 degrees F will only go 185 yards at freezing. Superficial heating does little good if the ball has been exposed to the cold over several hours. Heat three of four balls by setting them at the base of your kitchen freezer (where the warm air comes out) the night before you play. Then keep them in your hand warmer pocket and alternate them every hole. (When I travel by air and have to

A stocking cap, loose upper clothing, and rain pants kept this golfer warm.

play shortly after getting off the plane, I carry a sleeve of balls in my briefcase since those in the luggage compartment are exposed to extreme cold.) Just as effective in cold weather as in rain is the golf car cover that surrounds the whole car with four transparent walls. It will both shut out the wind and keep in the heat. Drinking warm liquids like soup, hot chocolate, tea, or coffee can help you retain body heat; but watch the caffeine as it tends to make one jittery.

Playing in the Heat

Very hot days can negatively affect your game just as well as cold if you are not prepared. The essentials that you will need to combat the heat are a broad brimmed hat (at the very least a cap or visor, although neither protects your ears or neck from the sun as well as a hat); U-V–rated sunglasses; sun screen with a minimum 15 protection rating; at least one towel; three extra gloves to replace those soaked with perspiration; and a water bottle. *I try to never pass an opportunity to drink water on the course, even on temperate days.*

Protection from the sun has even more to do with avoiding skin cancer than performance. Since golf is a game often played under intense sun, it is a problem to be taken very seriously. Still, don't underestimate the possibility of heat exhaustion, sun stroke, dehydration, or just plain fatigue in affecting your game. To avoid such problems you should be taking in liquids, preferably water or an isotonic drink rather than a carbonated sugary beverage. *Fi-*

Water is still best to drink on the golf course.

Isotonic drinks replenish liquid loss and have some nutritional benefits but are usually high in sugar.

nally, rule number one for your equipment in hot weather as in wet weather, is keep your grips dry.

Uneven Terrain

My experience tells me that fewer than 50 percent of amateur golfers understand the influence that uneven terrain has on ball flight.

Do this simple exercise to better visualize what happens once you discover that you are not living in a flat world. Hold your dominant open hand out in front of you so that the palm is flat and is facing an imaginary target to your left, like a golf green. Raise your hand six inches and the palm of your hand will still face the imaginary target; lower it and the result will be the same. Now go to the starting position again but tilt your hand backward, creating loft. Make the tilt resemble the loft in a pitching wedge. Raise your hand six inches again and see where the palm is now facing; markedly left of your imaginary green. Lower your hand and notice that it faces well to the right. This is precisely what happens to your clubface when you are on a slope where the ball is resting either above or below your feet. Although the leading edge of your club is still at a right angle to your target, the clubface is definitely not. This is true whether you are playing a full shot or a pitch. The ball will rebound off the clubface in the direction the face is looking. The more the loft, the more it will aim off line.

To adjust for this aim discrepancy I have developed a simple system. If you are on the course facing an iron shot to the green where the ball is above your feet, set your hand in front of you in a

Model your hand position to match the loft in the clubhead.

position that compares with the loft in the face of the club you are about to hit. Then raise your hand to match the tilt of the ground. Look in the direction your palm is pointing. Then rotate your body and hand until your hand, which is still tilted, is

Raise your hand to match the slope of the ground and see where the club points.

aimed in the direction of the flagstick. Your body alignment will definitely be to the right. You may want to allow for a slight draw as shots hit where the ball is above one's feet are more apt to produce that shape.

When the ball is above your feet, adjust for starting aim but also know that this lie will encourage a draw.

Playing Safely Out of Trouble

There are two shots that I learned relatively late in my career that have been very useful. My regret is that I didn't come across them sooner.

The first is the chip out. That may not sound too exciting but think of the many times you were in trouble, simply trying to play out to the fairway and then fluffed what seems a simple shot. Usually the conditions are similar to one of these. Your ball is in the woods resting 1. on loose pine needles; 2. sitting on ground with a sandy base; 3. nestled deeply in heavy rough. The cardinal mistake that is most often made in these three conditions is hitting behind the ball. Do it and the ball travels only a few feet, necessitating a repeat attempt to chip out and causing one more stroke to be added to your score. A very effective solution is to play the ball back farther in your stance than any shot you have ever hit, i.e., *slightly back of your rear foot.* Lean a little left, make no attempt in the swing to lift the ball up, and you will make solid contact with the ball (rather than hitting behind it), using whatever club you have chosen to escape your predicament. Use something like a 4 or 5 iron if you have to keep it low under branches, and a pitching or sand wedge

The secret to chipping out from a difficult lie is to hit the ball first, an action that can be encouraged by positioning the ball far back in your stance.

to come out of the tall grass if producing a higher trajectory isn't a problem.

Recovering with a Special Shot

Occasionally, you'll have the chance to produce a spectacular recovery. Such a time could be when you are in the woods and could chip out to the fairway, but instead you see a path through the trees to the green. The problem is that you are only 125 yards from the flagstick and would have to use a 3 iron to stay under the branches. How do you know how hard to hit a 3 iron and make it go only 125 yards? Let me explain how I do it, and then you can adapt the technique to match your own distances.

Normally I hit a full 3 iron 195 yards. When I lower my hands on the grip (choke down) by one and a half inches the distance, with a full swing, is reduced to 185 yards, gripping three inches down becomes 175 yards. Now I am at the lowest point on the grip, just above the steel. If I next shorten the length of my backswing (I estimate it to be about five inches) the ball will travel approximately 165 yards, five inches more 155, gradually bringing my arms down in those five-inch increments to 145, 135, and finally 125 yards! So I end up swinging with normal pace a 3 iron that is gripped down to

Knowing how to hit a long club short distances comes in handy when you are in trouble, and it will save you strokes.

the steel, using a backswing that has been shortened by 25 inches and I will get it very close to the green, sometimes on and sometimes even close to the flagstick. Course conditions will make a difference and may require you to make some adjustments. If the grass is wet and slow, add on some distance; if dry and fast, subtract. If it is slightly uphill add more backswing; downhill, subtract. Those things will be handled by your imagination. But try this technique and you will be amazed at how effectively it works.

Emotional Control . . . Using "the Next One"

At the beginning of this book we said that being in control was instrumental to good course management. That meant controlling the ball, controlling your decisions, but also controlling your emotions. In this series, the book *Mental Golf* provides a detailed system for developing greater mental strength, including ways to keep your emotions in check. But let me add a thought here that can truly help you with the emotional control aspect of course management.

Anger produces physiological responses that are frequently self-destructive when playing golf. We

Anger carried to the next shot is a tension-producing response, a negative for good golf.

all have witnessed and some have experienced the feeling of human rage that emerges when a person has hit a bad shot. I've seen players who have graduated from Princeton and gone on to Harvard Business School, yet out of anger over a mishit golf shot, announce to the world that they are "stupid idiots," as if their 135 I.Q. had just dropped by 50 points. Anger produces tension, and tension is the great destroyer of the freewheeling swing. So this is not a good course management response.

PGA Senior Tour professional Rick Acton uses an interesting approach to maintaining composure in such a situation. He says, "It is not the shot you just hit; that's over. It is *the next one* on which you should focus." Example: Your iron shot to the green fades far to the right, leaving you an almost impossible pitch. You play a lofted sand wedge to the fringe and the ball continues rolling across the green and amazingly drops in the cup. You see, it wasn't the weak approach to get concerned about but "the next one." Losing your emotional control over the first shot may have put you into a state that would not allow you to successfully produce "the next one." Ask Larry Mize if you don't believe its true. (Do you recall his fabulous winning pitch shot from the right of the green on #11 at the 1987

Davis Love won the 1997 PGA trophy after a near win in the U.S. Open the year before.

Masters to beat Greg Norman? It happened to be "the next one" after missing the green.) Acton recommends controlling those potentially destructive feelings during play by dismissing "this one" after it has been played, and focusing on "the next one." And why does this make such good sense? Because there is nothing that you can do about the last shot after you have hit it. The only thing you can do is to make a fresh start by focusing on the prospects of the next one being good.

Conversely, imagine that you have just hit a lovely shot to the green and are looking at a chance for a birdie. You may already be celebrating on your way to the putt. But then it takes you three putts and you bogey. You see, it wasn't the shot you just hit but "the next one." that should have captured your focus. Ask Davis Love, who suffered through this very scenario. He knocked it on the final green of the 1996 U.S. Open with a chance at a birdie putt to win, only to three-putt and lose. (The good news was that he came back to subsequently win the 1997 PGA Championship. In a sense, that was "the next one.")

Experienced players realize that golf is not a game of perfection. They are going to hit a certain number of bad shots a round. But the best performers do not lose composure when those shots surface: They just focus on "the next one." In this way they are in control.

Conclusion

As you have seen, there is a great deal to learn about being adept at managing your round on a golf course. It takes time and experience to learn the many nuances of conquering the challenges that golf offers. Even the most experienced players make errors in course management. Gary Player, for example, once mentioned to me that he made about five or six course management errors per round. How many then do you think you make? Certainly reducing the number would produce better scores. I leave you with a simple proven guide to put you on the right track. I call it the "Stroke-Saver System—Six Rules for Managing Your Game on the Course.

The Stroke-Saver System

1. I will use enough club on my approach shot to comfortably get to the flagstick.

Don't consistently come up short on your approach to the green; use enough club.

2. I will have a routine for every shot focusing
    on grip, aim, and setup.

Have a routine for all of your shots, including putts.

Having positive thoughts and seeing good mental pictures will allow you to make a more relaxed full motion swing.

4.   I will not swing with more effort than that which is needed to produce my effective swing speed (ESS). I will stay in complete control.

Finishing in perfect balance is an excellent sign that you have maintained your effective swing speed.

5. I will, when playing a full shot into the wind or to an elevated green or when chipping or pitching uphill, use a less lofted club; downwind, downhill, or to a lower level green, a more lofted club.

Downhill chips should be made with more loft, since the tendency is to be too long.

6. I will not leave makable putts short.

When in makable putt range, I always want to give the ball a chance to go in by at least getting it to the hole.

You will be surprised at how many shots you can save by simply applying the previous six rules as often as possible. It will take discipline and practice, but combined with the other information you have read, your scores on the course will definitely improve.

You will have become a good course manager.

All references to learning aids or practice devices can be answered at Golf Around the World, 1-800-824-4279, or at www.golfaroundtheworld.com.

Your Personal Course Management Notes

Your Personal Course Management Notes

Your Personal Course
Management Notes

Your Personal Course Management Notes

Your Personal Course Management Notes

Your Personal Course Management Notes

Your Personal Course Management Notes

Your Personal Course
Management Notes

Your Personal Course Management Notes

Your Personal Course
Management Notes